BOTH FEET ON THE LAND

INNERLIT STONE
www.innerlitstone.org

BOTH FEET ON THE LAND

FOUR SEASONS
OF CONNECTIONS AND REFLECTIONS
AT CREEKSIDE EDGE

NARAYAN

An appreciative shake to the helping hands
of the eight-armed goddess:
Tamara, Marilyn, Chetani, Marilee

Photography & Book Design: Narayan
Graphic & Photographic Production: Chetani McKinney

Innerlit Stone, Publisher
Nevada City, California, USA

Dialog from the Sierra Nevada
on Land, Literature, Art, Cultural Identity,
Inner and Outer Trails

www.innerlitstone.org

ISBN 0-9726857-0-7
LCCN 2003100032
Printed in Canada

Starting on the Same Page

Melting off the backbone to either side of our 400-mile-long Sierra Nevada, rushing between rugged ribs down forested flanks, lingering thru willow-lined banks into Great Valley or Great Basin— many of these watersheds contain a Deer Creek. Not such an imaginative name. Where else but browsing along a creek would the goldrushers and settlers expect to find lots of deer? And, for twenty years, i've found myself on this westslope foothill 'deer' creek; it doesn't matter which. Each is special. Each is crucial. Yet mine will never be set apart as a scenic monument, wildlife preserve or state park.

Did i arrive just needing quiet to pursue intensive study? to protect my own schedule? to pause a couple winters before my next move? At first, therefore, i flashed a scowl at the owner's few cattle, two goats, two sheep replaced by two pigs, occasional ponies, fluctuating mix of fox, bobcat, skunk and barnyard fowl. Suspicious of caretaker duties, cautious not to encourage dependents, i'd not be tagged a mister reliable putting out hay right on the hour. I'd not waste my time digging, weeding, picking, pruning. The furred and feathered types ignored my scowl— and waited.

Century-old apple trees bore fruit. Then with sporadic care, more fruit. Oh no! Wash, cut, knife ablur, on my feet all night long, kettles, bottles, 40 quarts boiled and sealed in 30 straight hours. Move away? New trees planted, rock walls built, debris fires, garden plots. Some co-dwellers departed, others arrived. Don't think i delivered the calf; mama cow had better know how. Raccoon, coyote and possum entered the game, and close up, two different cougars. This is whose property? I did refuse to pull porcupine quills from the new steer's nose. Yet rhythms of day and season permeated nerve fiber in ways that would seem familiar to our distant or recent ancestors. Step by step the land had taken me up.

Or, isn't it mind that takes up the land? Eyes ears opening to this place, opened by the power of place. Not mind as tangled snarled bramblepatch of me-mine, but mind as connective reflective flow into still pool. So, outdoor projects grew to balance indoor desk projects that my head-ucation had considered more important. Afternoon reading-writing moved outdoors, human trunk seated against oak trunk, pencil on pad. Reality buzzed, croaked and snorted in a world unpreoccupied with my preoccupations. Me-mine whirling in its own clever vortex does not receive what is.

If not unique, this creek's tinkling rumbling speaking waters are yet sacred. So is every place where teachers appear and needed lessons are taught. Do we not have to make special whatever place we now find ourselves in? This book does not promote any particular place; your own is where your answers lie. Quickenings may hit us quicker outdoors, when unwalled— but self-walled, we miss wonders of rainbow spray standing right under the most dramatic waterfall. My particular place has blessed me; i've blessed it.

So the poet sings the story of place. And it's not separate from the story of self. To single out highs or lows, to string together only extraordinary adventures one after another makes for exciting stuff. However, more transformative to us is the ordinary. Can the poet signify, clarify, intensify a succession of ordinary days, hours, moments? The storyteller in me, i admit, has not resisted including here some most unusual happenings. As a venture, tho, we engage the everyday, the actual world. Simple! Note it. Absorb it.

Yet what is termed 'poetry' in our language has come to mean an imagined realm, a personalized feeling-thinking space, a flight of fancy, a private dream. Questionable whether that sort of poet's place overlaps the reader's! We pore over it expectantly— uh who? where are we? what are the shared reference points? Then why am i trying to figure out this poet's fictive or even delusional world? So, contemporary poetry has earned a reputation as hard to decipher, vainly abstruse, or not worth an evening's baffled stare.

Here, this creekside world is not private. Its creatures are verifiable; its experiences are repeatable. Nothing is made up. Every experience occurred within a couple hundred steps of my cottage. I describe it as precisely as i can— within and without. Not altered to some notion of how it could have happened, nor retold as i would like it to have happened. Whenever in course of writing, i've got off track or stuck, my way forward has invariably been to go back. Revisit. If that scene or event is important enough to share, then every shimmer of leaf, every flicker of response is grooved exact in memory. What did happen? How did i feel? act?

These poems have been written over a period of twelve years (hermits love their penance), a few soon after the event, most years afterward from a note scribbled along the way. Worked at randomly one by one. Each 'final version' revised various times (now they really are final). So every poem can stand by itself; yet over the years emerged not a collection but a closely integrated cycle arranged spring to spring. It tells the seasonal story specific to temperate climes. And, if read in order, an oft-digressed but duly confessed people story: a man, a woman, synergies of approach and reproach, ecstatic gain, traumatic loss, a search for self in each other, a discovery of Her the Matrix who is desire's play and desire's end.

Let's agree, then, if we encounter root, rock, fruit or fuzzy foot, the subtext is our own body-mind-heart in relationship. With another, with ignored aspects of oneself, with Her in whom all appears. Our theme is not old-country activities and artifacts (nostalgia forbid), nor strategies for off-the-grid survival (go for it). Symbols and metaphors here do refer to mother-born nature more than surroundings man-made. Yet 'nature' not created by our plan can be found in any backyard. The full moon rises as the red sun sets— such facts never disappear. Other meaning-seekers may prefer a headlight, freeway exit, green-asphalted lawn, and graffiti on the dumpster. Whatever our situation, let attention do its work!

Why poetry? Isn't communication more easily made via diary page, sketch, pithy pronouncement, or selected essays? Maybe. Yet language which kind of indicates and sort of amplifies is soon forgotten. Why not value things said in a way that's worth memorizing? Cherish our experience recreated in the fewest strongest words? Condensed, focused. Like a laser beam, not a flashlight. Poetry is the means of transmitting the pilgrim's most memorable stages via memorable language. Chant penetrates more deeply than informal speech. Thus meter and melody in language cannot be obsolete. We've developed a tin ear; we read only discursive prose; we skim from headline to headline. Then, we honor as weighty the ponderous tome that failed to edit itself down to size.

In our postwar decades the mainstream of 'poetry' has eddied toward the discursive, the conversational. Ho hum, nice to hang out with friends— but is heroic utterance too much a challenge? Word-as-power not wielded to wake the brain? All obstacle-vanquishing chant lost in the past? Today's sprawling 'open form' of verse is merely prose typeset to look unlike prose. Where are its matching sounds? Any rhythmical motif? Any melody line sustained by long vowels? Intentional placement of strong syllables versus weak? Stanzas of a specific length that set the recognizable limits necessary to all art?

Poetry must be heard. Read out loud. Broadcast from toes thru tongue, then received thru ear into every cell. Or at least pronounced silently at speaking speed. If a passage offers only comment or anecdote without music, why consider it poetry? On the other hand, our complexities of psyche generate varieties of structure that do ask to be seen. The content must find a structure meant for itself; structure must facilitate and elucidate content. When both perfectly join, and the whole sounds utterly natural, as if it just fell ripe off a tree, then we have a poem that works.

Structure. Every poem here speaks in a specific meter of odd-numbered syllables per line: either 3, 5, 7, 9, 11 or 13. Whether a 'lyric' that evokes a moment or mood, a longer-line 'narrative' that tells a story, these meters help foster many rhythms other than the traditional iambic— for example, in "Outstanding," two different rhythms in the 9-syllable meter. Next point, meter is meaningless if it doesn't end with a completed phrase. And its beat slides past unnoticed if the line doesn't end with a strong syllable, or at the right instant a weak— for example, "The Talkfest." Next, single lines combine in couplet or triplet. These building blocks form stanzas of various lengths in a specific pattern— for example, "Midnight Flakes." No two poems have the same structure.

Photography. Looking thru a viewfinder may reveal a fresh angle; or it could restrict the ranging eye to a 35 mm rectangle. I had lived on this creek, in this cottage, for 15 years before taking my first photograph here. By then i should've known what to snap! Yet unexpected faces lurked in the tall grass; surprises jumped up in the process from lens to film to scan to page. Most of these photos occur within 200 steps of my door. I'm not a compulsive shutterbug; i may never take another photo at this place. Altho certainly not because there's nothing more to see! Drawing with light that's flaring, fading second to second, bursting on the other's face, bouncing back on my own— ever changingly new. And as we peer into thru behind our shadow play, each face is unchangingly Hers, each face is none but Her.

1

Seismic Stomp

Corner-cowed,
disavowed
any hunt,
peek thru bars,
wait for meals,
yawn and stretch
flatfooted,
snooze awhile,
stare glass-eyed,
whine in vain
for playmates.

How did i
so forget?

Sneak, shrink, squeeze,
maintain ease?
let old stuck
sense-benumbed
habits lie?

Or exert!
risk much hurt
to burst free—
had till now
wobble-prone
knock-kneed wish,
oft-sniffed hope,
fitful faith,
made some blood-
stirring swipes,
but where? when?
each moment
fierce intent.

How did i
so forget?

Crouch! don't creep!
clear outleap
those guardrails
learned by rote,
those fencelines
whip-imposed
or self-taught.

Shake the floors!
rattle doors!
back and forth
seismic stomp
this barred cage.

How did i
so forget?

Tail tip trained
left unchained
here's the chance
boldly seized,
here's the tool
to begin
my breakout.

Shrug off flaws!
sharpen claws!
all four paws!
roar loudly
right intent.

The Mother Space

Soon the air will fly with fluff
riding currents barely felt,
cottonwood soft floaty stuff
so lightweight each bit evades
any capture in closed fist.

Even if finger to thumb
try a pinch, it speeds off missed,
guarding that mysterious load
for landfall down vale unknown.

Inner-hid unique black speck
which path? hither thither blown
to chance on well-suited soil,
one near-invisible seed
potent with sky-spanning tree.

So puny a cause will lead
to such . . . ? No, nothing that small
could sprout an act or state big
as this wondrous-grown effect.

Soon every sprung shoot and twig
fill to edge the mother space;
mass of outspread glad-armed green
ever-twirling heart-shaped leaves
interbeam. Jai! noonlit Queen.

Splashed by dappling temple shade
we creekside creatures may sense
thru her overarching crown
something much more than immense.

Outstanding

Once lofty top knocked off by windstorm
just when it measured commanding height.
Maybe rose too fast, or aimed too big,
or ill-starred struck an unlucky stance.

Shows the most promise of all, they said,
in its grand shadow will many toil.
Destined, bred, sized for a king-like role,
now tho must serve only others' ends.

Growth long ceased, its furrowed bark slabs off,
bleached bare death offers a home for birth.
Nesting birds welcome a rookery trunk;
rodents get snug amid rotting roots.

Afternoon ramble thru open woods:

What's considered an outstanding life?
one's dream come true? master scheme worked out?
Fanfare greets those who attain the top;
no tribute heaped at a servant's feet.

At the No-Exit Spot

I can't! I can't!
shrill beseeching trembling squeal of baby red-tailed hawk
stranded at the no-exit spot. Nothing firm to grasp,
whichever side. Indignant skreak, disconsolate wail
I shan't! I shan't! Afraid to let loose, afraid to hold
at utmost tuft of tallest tree.

Come! Come! a cakewalk,
elders coax toward their perch on nearby pine. Now be bold;
show some spine! Once crawled scratching uptrunk from platform nest
to very tiptop, just flap one, two, three! Swoosh! Upsail
the ruffling draft, tingling airshine lifting buoyant chest;
enskied is our birthright.

Terrified, a tumbling gasp—
could first try fail? Life played safe doesn't stay safe? Wings unbound
must respond. No practice round. Whence unclung soaring flight?

From below i envy such drama at sun-blessed height
compared to stance in dullsville aground.

A Fat World's Mill

Loud crunches on the gravel—
the neighbor's truck off to work.

Sturdy stalwart young jobmate
methodical every step,
unvexed by the usual spate
of blueprints awry, on site
never absent, seldom late
in any kind of weather . . .

Loud crunches on the gravel—
the neighbor's car off to shop.

Tally up the per-hour rate:
that sum's quickly spoken for
just driving wheels round about,
plus food, clothing (to want more
of each is best), warm shelter,
taxes to fund this year's war

(sure! pay down the rich man's bill
while a fresh bone's thrown the poor).
Tuesdays the people go cluck
consent at the privileged few,
so that life shall stay (good luck!)
comfortably arranged in lieu . . .

Loud crunches on the gravel—
the neighbor's truck back from work.

Much grist for a fat world's mill:
at first glow who doesn't extoll
such pleasures as bow on cue?
then (so soon?) life catches chill,
ourselves thumped, stumped, too unwhole
to joyspend even one buck.
'Livelihood' in saxon tongue
meant venture-engaging thrill,
not the market residue
when x hours exchanged for cash . . .

Loud crunches on the gravel—
my hiking boots climb the lane.

Those whose work becomes a job
can afford both car and truck,
yet frayed getting ends to meet
may never afford a stroll.

I'm the sole neighbor who walks—
time is money. Let wheels roll!

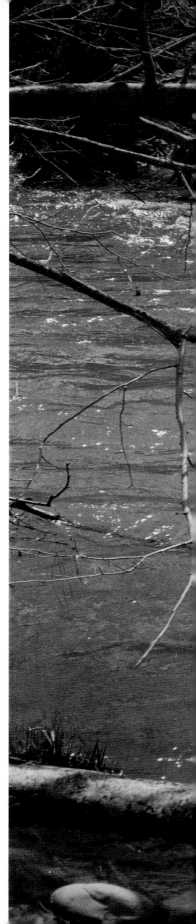

Competition

Creekside chamber choirs
carol, pipe, chirp, tweet,
twitter, chatter, coo
from before sunup
thru siesta hour
till after sundown,
even at midnight
warble, whoop, trill, hoot
in spring's round-the-clock
voice competition.

We marshmates hark dumb
at this wondrous din,
intimidated,
envious, awestruck.

"Their rules are no fair!"
bellows the bullfrog,
rasping grunts and kworks;
"let's disqualify
those melody-mad
meistersinger birds."

Chirk-squeaks the treefrog,
"Many types of song
do please diverse tastes;
the judges could vote
performance first prize
to us frogs on grounds
other than strict straight
standard bel canto"—
kwork— "there! coarsest croak!
or else let's declare
this contest adjourned
without a winner."

Fitted Rock

"Yes, my handiwork"—
proudly displaying two hundred feet of stacked dry wall
fitted rock by rock flat faced in double-terraced curves
against steep-cut slope. The nearly vertical chest-high
lower wall contains much boulder-weight lopsided stone
painstakingly lever-lifted and shimmed flush in line,
some split by sledgehammer blow yet seeming nature-shaped
eons ago and ever destined just to drop bomp!
in that exact place.

The biggest size outcropping chunks
had been bulldozed aside while scraping house pad and yard,
tugged, lugged, jammed in jumbled tiers. Assorted size picked up,
pitched up— yet rains arrive, banks do slide down— again mass
heaped huge load after load thru the homesteaders' draft-horse,
almost back-breaking years. Never scant harvest of rock
on this hillside. Each season one patch thoroughly cleared
sprouts rife from root a whole new batch. So my assigned task?
repile "permanent, with style . . ."

That jumbled tumbled hoard
a daunting sight. No ready-delivered neat supply
of square-edge rock easy to stack, no motorized aid
to help shove things about; only elbow grease attacks
the decades-crumbled tier, digs out what's here, uses up
every last skewgee bit. In this puzzle must belong—
days when set down once all facets fit; loose dirt flies fast,
whoopee! Other days not one rock meets another right;
biorhythms clunk, muscles crink; of course the elbow
tends to go kaput.

Began early spring, hopes ahead
of reasoned pace; summer turned autumn, finish! not done?
then many weeks' break as all the earthplay blocks lay low
too cold or wet to hold; resumed this spring. To avoid
hot afternoons i liked to wrestle rock by moonlight,
or shafts of porchlight, till one evening my battered spade
broke open an oval cave space. Dimly i could see
backfill seething and writhing vexed coils around both gloves—
a snake den! Lacking the lover-of-reptile's nerve quirk
i didn't grab ooh-aah, rather shoveled like mad, sprang back,
and swore off my night shift.

     Autumn, my handiwork done,
some visitor was admiring the new old stone wall:
"Looks nice. Quite a lot of rock to get brought in." Brought in,
dear guest! by contract with the local tectonic plate?
by starcluster clash? Resisting a pungent retort
i stood mumbling praise to our best, uh, only field crop,
then stepped aside. This incurious guest might next add,
"Amazing how all those rocks just fit!"

      Yeah, fit themselves,
they did, jump-bump bounced a lot splitting their sides in mirth
till each found its right place, then i chanced by to inspect
and approve. Ha! Ha! But don't grouch. No comment's inane—
in fact, laughs the gold-tinted land as i head downpath,
it's precisely the type comment i've earned and deserve
for proudly displaying "my" work.

Reluctant to Stop

Day's end, my brown pants browner with wholesome mud:

Nothing feels better than this quiet moment,
leaning on the door jamb, reluctant to stop
the digging, the transplanting, the partaking
in growth. Hands and feet have helped speed along spurts
green to gold, mauve and red— yes, every muscle
happily satisfied having flexed its tie
here to earth. Now step back; concede all control;
let others bud and branch their own varied aims.
Surveying my imprint on homescape, senses
filled with rocks and plops, worms and weeds, roots and leaves—
well done! Why, i'm not too tired to move more dirt,
work past sundown. Yet the conch blows. I must halt
for the day, heed the evening message, and stop.

Tunneled Under

The garden a maze of thieves' burrows,
dens and hideaways tunneled around
and under every edible root.
Despite dire warnings, deterrent wire,
traps poised, plus shrewdly placed poison piles,
monster incisors march on. The bloom
succumbs to dread chomp; the upright fall;
the good, grand or godly aren't immune.
One last scrumptious Easter lily bulb
shooting up all primed to announce spring—
resurrection dragged down inch by inch
for snacks in the gophers' heaving loam.

Jousting With Info-Glut

Manfully i charge the windmill, my pen held
like a lance leveled at rectangular foes:
tardy correspondence, old notes, unread files,

newsletters, magazines, contacts, connections—
jousting with info-glut, ho! Several high stacks
whirl a contemptuous blur on my too-wide desk.

Addled, muddled, unhorsed and forced to withdraw,
the valor-bent knight-errant has erred again,
mounted a frontal rush to sweep the whole field.

Um, i've tried commonsense advice. Sneaky raids,
reduce the stack page by page. Yet one if cleared
next day springs up two. An unwinnable fight.

Retreat, defeat— and the foe's merely paper?

Smoke drifting from the neighbor's yard cleanup fire
gives me a piquant clue, a twinge of glad hope—
too easy? or the needed solution? Yes.

Intentional Community

Recurrently, i attempt to find or form
a rural intentional community
(postfamilial pointing toward transpersonal)
to regroup myself in expanded matrix
where solidities intersperse oddities.
The flighty and the grumpy communalize
with even-minded head-of-the-table types;
we cross-fertilize but don't destabilize.
Interfaced, the peas must socialize with pods,
eugenically birthing a few wise youngsters
to utilize as interstitial cement
while co-building the rammed-earthen modular
interlocking planetary edifice.
Processing this proximity has its price:
continued deep intertouch demands we soon
should grind each other's long-sharpened edges off.

Gobble-Sure

After the first rain
when green tips begin to outcolor the brown,
here comes the turkey flock! Usually a farm
grows what the farmer may choose, but in our case
it's the wild turkeys who choose where best to grow—
and how! Egg to full weight in less than a year,
they outsize and outmaneuver the sheepdog
to roam as they please.
                Fine to see twenty strong,
meticulous at their housework, cleaning up
the property while storm clouds lift. Uh? They flap
over wire defense— what purposeful flat glide!
Next it's a systematic pick-and-peck tour
of my garden. All flint-eyed tough plants, tho yike!
big-beaked bodies ransack the mulch. Stems break off;
seeds and seedlings get unearthed, then tossed or stomped;
some few lacerated leaves outlast the raid.

To shout out irate's not enough. This could be
a question of us or them.
              Protrusive necks
promenade nearby, barely glancing my way,
so gobble-sure, disdaining strong-strung fencelines,
owner rights or appetites. Remember, yes?
wild turkey almost got chosen emblem bird
for this mighty nation, tho in retrospect
our forefathers did well to recast their votes
in favor of nobler profile, the hooked nose
of bald eagle now placed on coin and flagpole.

My point? Well, citizenship doesn't guarantee
the neighbors' toleration. Bob gobbler dares
fan his fat tail and strut his stuff all day long,
preen and pose for effect like a lion king
lounged atop the food chain.
            After many years
of mild mellow veggie fare, isn't it high time
i varied my diet?

Lonely

Wingtip to wingtip,
entranced antennae
in a pas de deux,
pairing swallowtails
flutter down the drive.

A third tries to join:
"No thanks! Flit away,
green-eyed chaperone."

Pause. Wing stroking wing,
on bud-burst lilac
two find the same grail,
toward one ambrosia
two strive, two arrive.

Wasn't it years ago
i learned not to feel
lonely? Just alone.

Fusty Patriarch?

Two ruddy-cheeked, glinty-chrome-clad drakes
pursue one duck— she skimming treetops, streaking averse,
they flapping like mad, both quacking appeal to halt now!
under next alder bough. Warm enough! Don't flee perverse,
join me! Or me! Choose which.

                              Scornful of their proferred tie
she zigs upcreek zags bye-bye. Her fault good looks entice?
tho speeds not quite resolved once for all to end romance—
some day to dally might be nice.

                              Fusty patriarch?
no no! I'm your dream spark! I can handle a dumped mood
or two, even help raise the first brood . . . Score? Uhh fat chance,
both splash down glum, shrug terse, commiserate— we're not flakes;
she could do worse.

Spaded and Seeded

Weeded, spaded and seeded—
i straighten up to adore
her willowy limbs, first-blush
warm skin, enigmatic smile.

Life juices rise, each stalk swells,
roots emboldened to stretch out
and clasp beneath polka-dot
covers of strawberry bed.

No urge to get up and go
stirs her procreant posture;
content and enceinte she lies
aglow, fragrant with semen—

the recumbent goddess Earth.

Chinaman

Buckets bob either end of a shouldered bamboo pole;
black pigtail bounces in breeze; efficient barefoot trot
crosses the grassy ranchland. Two more buckets of plops
reach the garden plot, to get soaked, set in sun to brew
fertilizer soup— he fed the rough new mining town
what veggies it ate.
> Altho Newtown's a century gone
the way mining towns go, leaving a ripple? a trace?
one burnt-down cabin's rock chimney to commemorate
the site? our neighborhood had managed to keep alive
its memory of this Chinaman, his master thumb
proving that nature plus human hand grows greener green
than mother nature left alone.
> Last summer, with spite,
i'd come to contrary thesis— lack of soil or thumb
leading me to conclude i'd better let nature grow
whatever nature can. My clevermost veggie plot,
promising most for least, was a mud strip in the creek,
ready with fail-safe water flow and annual flood
for nutrient return.
> The half-wild tomato vines
burst up lustily leafed; lots of little fruit set green;
fattened according to my best-laid plans; fattened more
to greener green. Then as nights turned colder, remained green;
autumn brought no tinge of red; winter saw that stone-hard
unmottled immutably green crop all swept away
in storm still unpicked.

I haven't discovered the true plot,
the Chinaman's fertile paradise. Where on these hills
could be loamy well-drained dirt?
                              His kinsfolk must have left
this area for citywork, many decades past
(local lore is vague on dates), and wouldn't have carried genes,
necessarily, for green thumb, nor continued well
the master's caring countrywork.
                              So our land endures,
his lineage ends— or may i tread firm in those footsteps
(with occasional stagger). Buckets full of cowplops
bob either end of a shouldered pole; hundreds of trips
crisscross ranchland to convert a small plot to farmland
(actually, not to the manner born, i found the pole
more encumbrance than aid).
                              Yes, i tried wheelbarrow power,
the home-built rumbler type. Too cloddishly noisy pushed
uphill. Simplest is best. One bucketful in each hand,
looking native in my own way. The west-slope foothills
are repeopled nowadays by every size, hue, caste,
class of hairdo (dyed, waxed, snarled, spiked), native fashion plates
imported from distant climes.
                              Thus a man's black pigtail
would look downright strait-laced to present taste, overprim,
old-maidish to young eyes, yet likely to occupy
a place of honor. I regret the master's not here,
invited to grace our land with silent step, find time
to tell us, if he would, what to plant? when? where? accept
cowplops in trade for seed? allow us to hoe his row?

and, if he were in secret a sage— point at the moon.

No Aptitude

Perfumed noon. On lavender spike bloom
busily proficient honeybees
chant self-content as they dip and sip
from brimful cup to next brimful cup.

By comparison a klutz, a clunk
deemed strictly unskilled labor unfit
for this dainty ambidextrous work,
one fuzzy yellow-black bumblebee
has wangled or forged a union card
to join the experts gleaning spring sweets.

Late sun thru whitish haze. Honeybees
all hustle home at approaching dusk,
while bumble toils till evening unfagged,
amassing gold pollen grain treasure.

Yet can this hard-won haul get airborne?
by textbook rule? there's slight or no chance:
bottom too broad, wings too short, hind legs
now overweighted with pollen globs;
in fact, an aerodynamic dud,
no aptitude for height. Some aren't meant—

hey! the damn contraption lumbers off
in slow spiral, slow but heavenbent!

Collecting what's been scattered afield,
inspecting complex mind's wayward tracks,
detecting long-forgotten treasure—
can't say i'm quite fit for this work.

Um. Slacked off. Yah, not when it feels time
some sunny day soon, not some full moon,
not even tomorrow, no delay!
no need to decide, the body knows
it must be today, now! I resume
my regular be-still sitting hours.

The Boy Remade Man

My entire boyhood
the wolves came prowling,
snarling, chasing me.

Down familiar streets
unrelenting fangs
nip snap at sure prey.

Glancing back at eyes
fiendish red, cold, fixed,
close, closer. Run! Run!

Over chainlink fence
across the playground
bare feet blur like wind.

Naked, unaided,
outnumbered, outflanked,
yet never outrun.

Right to my safe haunt,
trapped there, at wit's end—
then i would wake up.

In late teenage years
the same dreams resumed:
still the wolves pursue

over chainlink fence
across the playground
but meet a surprise!

Angry at running,
i stop, turn and face—
then i would wake up.

Later a third stage:
down familiar streets
running for dear life,

they hard on my heels,
drool-flecked fangs, red eyes,
easy prey. I stop.

I turn. I attack,
grab one by the throat,
lift up! smash him down!

The rest flee away
not once to return—
that dream brought an end.

The wolves prowled in me:
i set fear apart
but fear is myself.

If i don't disguise,
ignore, ennoble,
or seek to dismiss,

only then i face
me undivided,
one self not in parts.

The boy remade man
now could enter life
engaging it whole.

11

Inviolate Space

Midnight arrives warm:

Hatched out resolute
converging in droves,
filing up the walls,
scouting the windows,
seizing the least crack
and squeezing inside,
earwigs infiltrate
my tight-sealed thick-walled
inviolate space.

This villa i rule—
mine by right and might!
stuff and self arranged
just so, nicely kept.
They! They perch, wedge, traipse
on in under shelf,
drawer, stove, rug, desk, dish.

Smite! Smite! Wipe 'em out—
from hat, shirt, sock, bed!
Yet as housemates go
i have to admit
their habits are mild.
At least they don't gripe,
slam doors, lose my books,
teevee my airspace,
don't slop up the sink,
filch much from the frig
nor ask for cash loans.

No definite threat—
despite wicked look
those pinchers won't pinch
unless sorely pressed.
Come to stay? pass thru
without right of way?
okay, let 'em be.

Warm nights always bring
crowds out for a stroll.
Better share our space,
engage innerwork,
postpone the campaign
to exterminate.
Not that i'm disarmed—
don't claim to love 'em
but it's not yet war.

So Near

Oh-i ku, ku, ku,
drawn-out receding
melancholy call.

Midsummer where are
the prevalent jays?
forthright screech Ksh ksheek
unclouded by moods
overemphasized
to reactive spin.

Instead, flocks of doves
roam the hill sighing
at love's labor lost.

Their soft ku, ku, ku,
should feel more soothing—
yet blue-sky days pass
in vague disquiet
that a friend so near
sounds so far away.

Name-Tagging

Much-thumbed species-complete identification guide
in hand that lists and labels thy size, shape, sex and song,
seasonal hues, habits, diet, home range, . . . that describes
concisely all things describable, specific marks
and traits distinguishing thy kind from like-coiffured kin,
discrete parts and particulars analyzed and named
to help me see difference.

Um, pondside views blur today;
please don't shy back in cattails, i'm not binoculared
nor otherwise armed, dear phoebe, or is it pewee?
certainly not high-country blue grouse, and i should hope
not killdeer the cousin of killjoy? nor shrill-note shrike,
abusive thrasher, nor meek mild co-dependent thrush;
and be assured, never would i measure and judge thee
a poorwill, much less a titmouse! Rather fine mood boost
if meeting jaunty junco or virile vireo,
yet here it says call thee old coot.

So, so many names,
minutely drawn details, hugely massed data compiled
to acknowledge the wealth of variegated forms—
tho once pursued this passion for difference now obsessed
with name-tagging each of you, do i better commune?
or does not mind filled with many tend to disengage
from the all-indwelling One?

Big raucous crested jay
swoops down to confront me eye to eye. Ah! views break clear:
not defined by identification, not described
by list and label abides thy identity state,
pure I-dentity indescribable— like my own.

She Is

Lotus feet submerged. Ease-filled gaze cast-on-all-the-same
reflects off rippled sheen. Long skirt hitched up. Her free hand
outflung toward balance point darts and dives as if to stitch
together whole each ragged-torn piece of sky and earth;
teetertot she skips downcreek on algae-coated stone
smoothed round by geologic grind.
                       One instant slips, ooh!
nimbly rises dripping from ocean depth, clinging cloth
molded close on eye-seizing goddess form, the Ur-Form,
the Origin made flesh, the Sum birthed to hold two-armed
all desirables most desired. Day-outsparkling Bright
not displayed but whimsically disported; somber Truth
that has no shape-age-name, the No-Form, here shaped and named
and almost near enough to touch.
                      Twice? Thrice? We had met
occasions past. Greeted. Spoken. Did blinds lift a crack
striving lifelong to attend her Gaze? Yet only now
between alder-lined banks did i see direct, entire—
see undistorted thru fogged lens of embodied state
to what she is— She Is that self-as-world veiling force
whose sight makes clear one in all.
                       Her insouciant big toe
doodles in sand: First a single dot, then lines outreach,
intersect, join three sides, amplify, triangles point
down and up, worlds superimpose on worlds. Awe-engaged,
she contemplates her geometry of womb-delight,
her power to create.
                  Creekside, no words exchanged. A sight
offers, enters each eye, goads, coaxes, maddens each sense
to keen expectant edge; grants the focused means to see
my own mind-heart-stuff arising subsiding in Her,
each torn piece of sky and earth churning as Her. She smiles;
her foot sweeps the sandbar. Evidence is bit by bit
erased— but not altogether. I've been shown what's what.

Escapes, Rescues

The hawk swoops from vantage perch behind a trunk;
two dozen quail scatter— one hits the wire fence,
falls to ground, fights a few minutes against fate,
then lies still. The hawk's glide swerves over driveway
past its prey; turn round? it may, for picnic lunch;
or if not, the circling vulture, sniffing fox,
bobcat, scavenger ants . . . Life is not a waste.

Yet i want to run help, reverse the mishap,
not stand detached, observe— but act, intervene,
swagger up! A Protector God doing good
in response to poor quail's prayer, righting what's wrong
with its world, then awarding merited boons
to all concerned. Except here, specific case,
help whom, quail? hawk? and how make the outcome just?

Well-flown escapes often fail, planned rescues too.

Four Arms

Full moon close above,
rustling pines in rows.

A dance unbegun
occurs unannounced,
proceeds unrehearsed,
four arms round one trunk.

Straight and strong that life
swaying as one spine
in surge without end.

No patterns preset
for first step or last,
no programs planned out—
as is, we're achieved.

Hooting owl peers down,
cat waits on doorstep.

Rush for Refuge?

Downhill toward the pond, a sharp left near the creek
where barbwire fence ends, three steps thru clover smack!
my foot square on rope-like thing two inches thick
that wriggled, jerked, sped—
                              left me hung in midair
with sandals taken flight in opposite arcs,
hung up there quite some anxious while! breath indrawn,
till i spied (much relief) his tapered tail tip
disappearing in rush for old refuge hole—
a fat gopher snake, seldom surprised by day,
unlike the sun-flopping nap-prone rattlesnake
marked indistinguishably in this locale,
each with bold geometric diamondback strip
tho heads and tails contrast.
                              Breath outblown, descent
unshod to ground. I'd been long taught to beware
the fat rope mistaken for illusive snake,
yet how prepare to see the other way round?
very unfake five-foot-long snake mistaken
for rope or pipe.

Odd, i wasn't alone. Right hand
on her bare forearm, engrossed in talk (the scene
those few seconds before midair shock appears
clearly once more), gazing back holding her gaze
as i turned thru deep rose clover, two steps, three . . .

Interpreting signs? Not a snake in tall grass
feigning friendship while plotting treacherous deed!
no, i sense a different kind of snake at large,
benign but not boxed-up tame, poised to begin
its work, coiled as fearsome force at base of spine
ready to strike at heedless companionship
that seeks escape from sorrow, boredom, despair;
restless companionship that can only skid
getting-to-know-about-you slushy byways,
indulging 'needs' to possess and be possessed
at mutual encampment.
                          Hand on forearm,
yet never glued face to face! not crammed alike
two per can. Rather, room provided to roam,
to grow unique, to meet each in egg-shaped space
that coiled-up snake whose implosive strike undoes
misheld misconceived 'needs'.
                          What if we should touch
not as pattern-pat personhoods issue-stuffed?
touch not to weld one tight gear-meshing device
from pairbonded selves? but to recognize One
manifest as two— like those sandals well matched
winging separate tho complementary arcs
over bramble patch, retrieved and soon rejoined
one per foot to share unshaken wide-braced stance
in open air under vibrant blue expanse.

Is there such need then to rush for refuge hole?

Ancient Gods

Wilting early summer heat, fifth year of basic drought:

The dust lies deeper each hot spell; the biggest gray pine
dies from top branch down; the once frolicsome creek shrinks back
prematurely running bald; each cell that tries to swell
in dayshine dries out— this entire wizened earthling world
needs a good soak.
                 Sure! a good soak. After the solstice
when rain can't fall here? Cloud long since flown to other clime,
our wet season's passed. A few localized thunderstorms
could hit high on the crest, but for hill creatures too bad,
summer rain never falls here.
                 At the calm evening hour
we sit and chant: "Below! Above! Beyond! That, the Source,
the illuminating Sun," as he flattens down red
on vast pacific waterbed, "the Truth we adore
and contemplate; may It enlighten our questing hearts"—
recited three times, while unnoticed, a louring west
gathers breadth above the far shadowy coastal ridge,
spills over the central plain, and noiselessly piles dark
up foothill slope. Thick blanket at day's end? A cloud front
after the solstice? Rain can't fall here.
                         One minute, look!
given desperate thirst, we vainly self-sufficient folk,
often common-sense deficient, why not call for help?

call on all cells' behalf. Invoke nature potentate
Indradev, the rainmaker. Stand! Urgently invite
this much-ignored tho in bygone times exalted god
to come bestow downpouring grace.

View ocean's extent
beyond frothy foamed beach: with voracious slurp fill up
distended belly huge, our needed water contained,
pivot west to east across farm plots and peopled lots,
picture the great-peaked backbone range stretching south to north,
and spray out wetness its entire thirsting length. Rain can't
fall here? Why not? Bring it by clear intent; focus mind
unhurried; visualize results. Tho calling for help,
feel oneself to be the potentate called. Then repeat,
three times is enough. Not too much. Drench, don't flood away!

Silence. Fatigued creatures hush. Some slight peculiar sense
of world's breath in suspense— what next?

Drops begin to splat,
fat drops on accumulated thick dust, weighty plunks,
not just a sprinkle, a full storm. Our conch shells blow thanks!
bent pines on parched hills dance with unstarched glee. A new lease,
a second chance! The lame trickling creek gulps to unshrink;
thru thirty-odd hours rain pelts down hard; shriveled-up cells
washed fresh, each swelled out and twice blest. Jai Jai Indradev!
our brains will resprout.

Forces embodied, ancient gods
are not dead; they wait in exile, wait for the instant
we arrogant moderns call Help! Come get reinvolved!

Outside Door

The outside door at my place
shows unaccountable moods:
willing, then recalcitrant,
works properly, then it quits.

Stepping in out all day long
i should know its every quirk;
we've been with each other years.

Maybe when too dry? too damp?
suddenly it doesn't quite shut.
Push! It bounces back unlatched—
bothersome, the stubborn thing,
exasperating, perverse.

I slam it hard and harder;
compelled, it can't fail to shut!
An inexplicable bounce—
it refuses to be forced.

Yet a soft supportive touch,
a kindly nudge with a twist
latches it shut every time.

A slam can't fail to shut it;
no way a nudge will shut it!
where the? against all reason
why does? how can it behave
opposite to how it should?

Uh! Stop. Rewind. Don't spin mind
speculating on first cause,
likely motives, maybe, if,
why? how? Just be with the fact.

Often tactics need review:
there could come a time to slam
but right now master the nudge.

This Twosome

Sunset sitting time: Rouge fire beds down
steaming western seas; the azure dome
shades to solemn iridescent hues;
low-swung peeks the shiny sliver face
witness to rarely neared sun-spun trails.

Just above the tips of hillside oaks
two steady beams out bright before stars;
Venus, the love-waking potent charm,
and Jupiter, the truth-pointing thrust,
orbit in tandem close to caress.

Sadly, star charts tell they'll next approach
this consenting in two hundred years,
ten generations! Bad news, i say,
for love to fly off disjoined, bereft,
holding back fond floods not yet expressed;
and for truth to withdraw mute or moan
his thwarted verve racking to sheer rage.

Passion Wisdom, what an ideal match!
why is't not fated to last?   The stress,
we hear, incarnating love or truth,
the pressures— and Mars owns a big house
right down the road, Vee's option for sure;
besides, tho keenly regardful now,
Jupe will soon be wanting his own space.

So, attend their benefic bliss-bond
while they yet adore, this week merge rays,
truth enfolded by unfolding love,
trade sweetmeats, endearments, glowing gaze,
enraptured clasp— before linking up
becomes work, kiss turns to arm's-length hiss,
cloud nine goes poof! then therapy hours.

Sitting time ends: O twinkling Skywheel!
o night-illuminating Fatewheel!
reveal the innerbonded mind-space
where wisdom is act and passion state,
object not other than subject self—

this twosome one compassionate Void.

Young Kitty's Case

                    Sleek slinky silky shape,
lustrous black black tho with reddish tinge,
and two white whiskers.
                          Adroit stalker,
adept leaper— supposed to live fierce,
relentless, remorseless, and throw dread
into rodentdom.
                No, stay outside,
even if lonely on coldest nights,
dear garden guardian Kali Kitty,
golden-eyed huntress.
                  In recent weeks
i've had to get on young kitty's case,
in fact even yelled when she curls up
sleeping complacently thru the night
like a degenerate couch cushion
sated on sissy food.
                  Killing fields
await! Grim-reaper traits honored here,
not this fluffball persona. Don't snore
life away! Get up and hunt at night;
that's when the gophers come out, i know,
and wrapped in black coat on a black night—
hapless prey!
                  Ignoring my counsel
she grows alert only at noontime
to the munchable rustle bustle
busy building tunnels. Without tools
to dig them up, every hunting trip
ends with a futile empty-pawed pounce
at a swaying stalk.
                No, Kitty, no,
it's after sunset, after midnight
when milksops are in bed, only then
the gophers come out.

Today at noon
Kitty appears thru the oaks, arched brow
triumphant, with a still-warm gopher
dangling from her mouth.
                              Strut and loud purr
so there! before settling down to lunch
on the front porch. Crack crunch celebrate
Kitty's own original technique
that shouldn't work. Must be beginner's luck
or a specially stupid gopher—
look, i know what i know.
                              The textbooks
agree that gophers come out at night;
besides, long ago i was close friends
with a half-wild mama cat. She was
a champion huntress and taught me—
not that i grabbed any bare-handed
but i knew her habits well. She caught
her gopher meals always in the dark;
once teaching her kittens how to hunt
brought home three in one night.
                              Days later
again at noon, again strut and purr,
with a disdainful leave-it-to-me
lifted paw, the huntress Kitty drops
a second gopher, certified warm,
at my ever-disbelieving feet.

Okay, okay, i'm getting the point:
not to be circumscribed by what's known
of world and self, to encounter now
what's truly new, i must first realize
i don't know.

Error of Scale

Pitch dark under the great curvy-limbed gray pine
out my back door. A single satisfied grunt
from the first-time mama cow, an easy birth
achieved. Now Junior enjoys day two's routine,
dozing most hours in shade but when thrust afoot
quite able to follow Mom around.

"Come look!
Kitty, meet our wee calf," i call the black cat
into the pasture. She slips thru knee-high grass,
innocently stealthy, pads pantheresque, poised—
till spied by mama cow. "Humf!" Twelve hundred pounds
charge against twelve, charge at this predator threat
stalking her young.

Just a slight error of scale
determined by program laid out in the genes;
each circuit perception to reaction (click!)
still not adjusted to actual-world size,
despite a thousand generations since Moo
became a huge hulk and Meow a minimuff
who stalks handouts from a bag.

Core change occurs
not by passage of time! Solely by mind flame
unstoked with mind's fuel— piercing wide-shining rays
that illumine unshadowed all sides at once,
the brain field's entire program cause to effect,
stimulus response. Then might a new-found mode
see direct the thing-as-is free of one's past.

Securely Zipped

Cool summer night
at stillest hour, night's dead stillest hour:

Securely zipped in dew-shedding bag
on the low front deck, the shrunken creek
a murmur merged in dreamless deep sleep—
Aii! Aii! close, a loud scream, louder Aii!
quivers quavers— Aii! rips thru the cloth
wrapped round my ears against chill.
                                      Breath halts,
blood throbs, hair jerks on end— one more scream,
i never have nightmares? right close by
sounds like, must be a terrified wail,
a woman hurt, attacked— tho i hear
no definite cry "Help!" as dazed nerves
regather and recall how to sit,
my shook-open eyes cautiously peer
over the rail.
                    There! three bounds away,
broadside in moonlight, come-hither tail
swishing wishful, self-preoccupied,
a roving female cougar howls yowls
to locate a compatible mate,
ignores me! crosses thru barbwire fence—
minutes pass, the same uncanny wail
uphill, more wails five hundred yards off
continue her rapt neighborhood search—
whew! i'm not it.
                        She might've caught a whiff
of me. Inferred not her type. Indeed!
not the staunchest partner tried and true,
yet playspace, creekside view, sleeping bag
could spread out for two, life sizzle new—

whoa! She herself tires of fervent growls,
bites, scratches, persists at most six weeks,
then it's evident our gifts, needs, goals
can not be reconciled.
                              Self-esteem
may droop when passed by. Yet praised be peace!
this heart's not built to withstand the wail
of wounded-woman ills— makes me feel
obliged to jump quick and give relief,
scurry after some cure, soothe her ache,
fix her pain, fix it! And who can fill
such shrieking screeching want?
                              Left alone
i lie back again, securely zipped
in throat-snug bag on the low front deck,
and soon sink down whorls of scene, event,
response, result to dreamless deep sleep,
then wake at sunrise my normal way:
long-drawn breath, tranquil vein-coursing blood,
hair smooth, no alarm.

Reddest Bloom

Evening, under the live oak,
as songbirds rustled to roost,
she lay serenely curled up,
even her wakeful ears slept.

Stride softly, don't startle her—
but when i passed by next day
she hadn't stirred. Glossy fur dull,
dim, diminished by sunforce.

Into a large wheelbarrow
i heaved her (is't still a her?
dreadful smell, maggots at work),
rolled downhill to the garden,
dug a pit in sticky soil
where my load tumbled, remained
under fresh-spaded bare mound—
one doe serenely curled up.

Ten feverish furious days
flies hatched buzzing from that mound.

Now hollyhocks rise rejoiced
in healthiest reddest bloom.

One Thru-Flow

Shut-off space
constricted
conflicted
breath all stuck.

One slight wisp
of wild wind
tries to slip
past the knot
in each cell
where clinched clenched
will to feel
affected
connected
wrestles roused
to breathe dead
out, live in.

How assist?
gently urge
rhythmic flow
to unclutch—
thy outbreath
i breathe in.

Bottled up
where's the cork?
pain-squeezed eyes,
prickle-pin
lips, clamped jaw,
stiff-ribbed chest
works to coax
inflated
pulsated
cloud expanse
belly broad
deeper down.

Surely air
never lacks—
thy outbreath
i breathe in.

Grasping gasp
clutches throat,
muscle cramps
damp air flow,
finger claws'
iron-tight
stranglehold
grips against . . .

Good! Inhale
each knot loose—
thy outbreath
i breathe in.

Raspy aarwk!
assisted
untwisted
something gives—
jaws ease up,
claws uncurl,
heart-burst zing
cracks in bits
armored shell,
fresh force floods
pelvic floor
to far toes.

Unshut self
free released,
one thru-flow
who always
was complete
aware space
that's been lived
as mere parts—

the full-breathed
all-healed Whole.

III

Each Time Round

Another birthday.

Time's fleeing, they say,
off like a straight shot,
yet why not chasing?
chasing its own tail
with me hanging tight
to lash-happy tip,
counting each time round.

Not a cute kitty
chasing its own tail,
rather a cougar
with jaws meant to crunch
when it catches up,
as it surely must
some sunshine day soon.

So, lashed round and round,
let me snaggle-smile
wide open at heart,
stride free of tight-assed
oft-contorted gait—
then die ever young
as old as can be.

Cocky Command

While still dark, cocky command Up Sun!
from chest outpuffed, tail fluffed, here's the man
who brings on light if anyone can
arrange such. Up Sun! Rise at full run . . .

how nice, known day routes resume the same,
tho compared to dream scene rather lame . . .

insistent summons, predawn alarm
means to shake tumble forth leg and arm,
propel far fast from laggardly daze
into press-the-pace action-packed ways . . .

oh no! not yet! I squirm deep in bed;
harshly lit should's crowd close overhead . . .

his rule despotic as grandpa clock
unless— unless tonight? equinox,
season's end, timeshifter trickster fox
comes to throttle that doodle-doo cock.

But Brief

The pasture parched, eaten down,
only a hose-watered patch
shows green recycling from brown.

No burdensome chores or tasks
for the turbo-chomping steers—
just keep my corner patch mowed.

Day done. How about our wage?
curl raspy tongues thru the fence—
short on cash, two apples each.

They smell i'm an orchard man,
so this hand is safe to lick—
it won't take back what it gives.

Dolce vita, life tastes sweet,
tho a penalty's to pay—
growth so sleek, so quickly plump.

Go, masticate the good life,
make a munch of one last month—
scenes are lovely here, but brief.

Autumn's First Touch

After a prolonged summer
whose balminess felt secure,
all at once autumn's first touch:

Midday breeze hinting at bite
startles the complacent neck
used to languorous caress;
clat-clattering crisp brown oak leaves
tap cross-rhythms on the roof;
twirling spear-like pine needles
peril the butterflies' path.

Dust whoofs up in tingly air
that's trying to recollect
how months ago it made clouds.

Not like winter's plaintive blasts
wailing lonely thru bare limbs,
these puffs cavort with leaf toys
to yo-yo and toss aloft;
but somehow seem reflective
rather than beach-weather blithe;
autumn sees its play soon spent.

Is't gain for the single leaf
to blow off quite last? Should wind
post us all a waiting list?

Not to get disturbed, be left
unconsoled, we crave answers
faithworthy, foolproof, set firm;
yet in questions well pursued,
in the courage to let go
our most enshrined convictions
is found truthfulness and truth.

Heron House

Afternoon of the moving day. Lift, lift, now unload,
bend, bend, position knees under dead weight, set it down,
there! straighten up. Face about. Keep good cheer. Next box, next—

skree-aawrk! Ear-discombobulative low-altitude
sound-barrier-obliterating screech-engine salute,
its wingspan rip-roared shadow huge over the front deck
where my boxes were stacked, a table, two chairs, some boards
for bookshelves. A modest pile pleading to get unpacked—

as i jerked up, wouldn't have been surprised to see him leave
a contrail at head height. Hey! I'd just dismissed the truck,
dismissed the road. Belongings now belonged to one place
after long years dispersed. Objects a swirl. Yet i'd soon
make order here, unbundle, assemble, sort and stash—

don't get overwhelmed. The new place. Not quite called a house,
something between cottage and cabin, but civilized
by water that runs, lights that switch on, all-weather drive
(embarrassed how close to town)? Even telephonized
for local-acting, global-thinking citizenship—

not yet emptied the first box. That roof-rattling flyby
sheared so low i had to duck. His guttural squawk Hi!
aggressive-hearty, hale-intentioned, and perfect-timed
welcoming the new kid on creek. Tho, ehh? a prelude
to like salutes? No, he never buzzed my deck again—

by nature and circumstance withdrawn, the hermit type,
born untouched by party proclivities. Years before
his wife-for-life had been shot by a teenaged shithead,
then, i'm told, outraged neighbors felled the teenager's dog
(frontier justice, if not for the dog). Heron, great, blue—

altho i may be closest surviving kin, he keeps
enough distance, i can't verify the color blue,
rather gray, i'd guess. But great? Ho, standing four feet tall
with wingspan to dwarf mine. Sunset like a scheduled gong
he rasps aawrk! aawrk! flaps departure from his creekside realm—

it's warmer to spend nights uphill. At sunrise he's back
fast on a favorite rock midstream, ruling the small raft
in the duck pond, surveying mortal merry-go-rounds
high from cottonwood limb, or poised in reeds, half-closed eye
sizing up frogs that populate the edge of our deep—

zap! Faster than thought. Stab. Gulp. Poised again. The old monk
will stand hours on fixed leg, balanced, patient; knows to let
surface what must surface, not to push rush an outcome
toward self-gain. Easeful yet attentive, not tensed to aim,
thus free to strike unerring when the instant arrives—

lost art of timing. If he should once miss (any act
can fail in planned result), he waits until the mud clears,
wastes no emotion-energy in shore-thrashing moves
that will further obscure, cultivates one-legged stance,
and watches the object reappear. Unerring aim—

easeful's not easy to do. Local? Global? Be still
until the right moment resolves action to sure act.

79

Tall Tales

We were sitting on the patio
at storytelling hour, boy all ears,
grandfather wonder-tongued.
                      Pappy hailed
from a region of the continent
that claims to specialize in tall tales—
each taller than the last, campfire-spun
ages ago, or perhaps composed
right on the spot. He would begin slow,
poker-faced, with merry wry twinkle
reflecting southwest sky in blue eyes:

Sunset. A hunter came stalking deer
down a sparsely wooded ridge. To take
only one two-point buck per season,
allow himself only two shots, fixed
was this personal rule. Never once
had he failed, in fact, to hit the game
held in his sights his very first shot—
until that evening.
                   Browsing alone,
there! a gigundous stag (tens of prongs?
mule deer can't reach near such bulk) paused still,
backlit broadside, nonchalant, assured,
fifty yards across a rough ravine;
too big, too old for the hunter's need
but too tempting a trophy. One shot
couldn't miss. Bang! No response? The second—
this lordly stag glanced up unconcerned
and grinned. Frustrated, his two shells spent,
the hunter thrust deep in coat pockets,
pulled out something hard, loaded and fired—
a dry old peach pit. This time the stag
flipped a somersault, crashed thru dense brush,
then disappeared.

Next autumn, returned
again to these parts, searching all day
for his usual bag, one two-point buck,
the hunter was scanning a meadow
one hundred yards downhill. Nothing stirred
attracting keen eye. Suddenly, tho,
near his elbow, it seemed! a few twigs
pop-snapped. By instinct he leapt, whirled round
face-to-face with— yep, that very same
gigundous stag grinning a welcome
friendly as could be. Yet, fading light?
what didn't look right? Lush foliage rose high
vibrant green, foreign to scrub oak hills—
well, i'll be! Easy-like, the stag bore
a full peach tree rooted on his back!

There, as i recall, the hour-long tale
ended, not with moral or maxim,
nor today's popular 'ology
presenting the psycho-mythic keys,
ugh! that we should keep twisting in mind—
just pure story.
                Pappy would chuckle,
an instant or two his gaze intent
under that blue twinkle, long enough
to let me suspect his tale meant— what?
need versus greed, death producing birth,
the Tree of Life?
                Yes, it wasn't his style
to break down simple tales (leave 'em tall,
taller, and tallest!) by heaping up
stiff overweight stentorious purport;
anyway, all interpretive slant
we soon forget; commentator's gloss
each generation invents anew.

The story stands on its own as true.

In Pursuit

With such nimble feet and thought
we chase after what we want!

In the pasture on steep slope
a big apple-laden tree:
Climb cautiously, crane way back,
clear-picking to fill cloth bag;
my hefty chums crouch and watch.
Some few sun-juicy red balls
tumble off and bounce downhill;
three steers upspring in pursuit.
Fifteen hundred or so pounds
turn alacritous lightfoot
leaper unstoppably loosed;
low-throated growl of delight
rather feline than bovine
chases pounces on his treat.

Too bad the apple i chase
cannot be had by a pounce.

The Longer Reach

When picking, tho i may hum or sing
and look plan-free, i'm systematic,
even aerobatic in the tree,
collecting every single last fruit—
the bird-gashed, the worm-bored, the deer-gnawed,
off-colored, lopsided. All get used.

Those left up high? No, no i didn't miss;
rather, i couldn't reach them. Or— could have
yet don't feel today i had to reach
so high. Call it shortage of skill? will?

Yes, we've urge to extend, to exert
the longer reach, then the tighter grip;
however, i'm learning not to strain
for each outermost limb, nor expect
to pocket every fruit. To grasp less
might be to receive more—
                                          and those left
will be enjoyed by creatures on wing.

Stern Consequence

Near dark i duck
past the century-old apple trees
and hurry down the row of gnarled vines,
peering poking for nectar-ripe grapes
to sweeten my twice-a-day herb drink,
altho birds . . .

Ahh! Here's a bunch unpecked,
kept hidden by close-knit leaves. Quick toss
into mouth. Yum. Muscats are quite mild
compared with concords. More tosses gulped—
uh-oh! My satisfied smile contorts,
heart sinks to heels. A foolish mistake
gobbling fruit not yet ripe!

Notice why
the birds left this prize beckoning bunch
for next week! Even born ironmen,
innards cast unetchable, don't mess
with sour grapes. Pick them whitish not green!
distinctions oft ignored. Thus desire
goes awry.

Choice: to take or to wait,
wise birds get it right. Outside my door
in the live oak they perch, settled down
fluffy to sound sleep, free of regret
or stern consequence. I'll turn in late
with a bellyache.

No Right System

Brambly patches, bristly untrimmable hedge,
enticing fruit i can't ignore— but be warned!
there's no right system for picking blackberries.

One object, various methods. Deer stretch out necks
nibbling the perimeter, skipping the rest;
so i follow, doubly clothed. Yet no armor
can prevent scratches! Ankle, wrist, elbow, knee,
then juice and blood paint hands a distinctive hue.
Of course, rubber gloves— harsh unrelenting thorns
poke straight thru. Why not quit now? Or leather gloves—
no more pricks but my fingers can't feel the fruit.

Next, i try laying eight-inch-wide boards on top
to foray across the outermost defense;
this stratagem will surely outwit the vine.
Uh, embattled language oozes from my wounds,
as i creep precariously gaining midpatch
where purplish booty hangs ripe. I must have it!
Imagine bowlfuls. Here any effort's worth—
only don't plummet into thick waist-deep thorns.

Sometimes, when my incursions by land fall short,
i withdraw to the rowboat and launch upcreek
to attack at rear where the most luscious plump
berries dangle unfortressed over water.
Pole along expectant, but the boat drifts back,
again the fruit out of reach. Or snatched at— lurch,
teeter, left fist clutches thorns, ow! loud splash. Damn!
one picker soaked, one best bowlful spilled downstream.

The scratches will heal. Once frozen or bottled,
winter eating's a joy. Yet i do admit
there's no right system for picking blackberries.

The Talkfest

Scheduled every fall
after the first freeze,
hundreds congregate
in the dead gray pine—
extensive seating,
each perch with clear view.

Like-feathered share tell
the latest and best
in raucous review
daily for a week
or two till quite stuffed
with the evening news.

Right as flattening Sun
signals calm, erupt
tonight's episodes
chirped tutti, loud, fast,
each voice exultant
as chief raconteur.

Stragglers rush beaks cocked
to foist off advice;
a clique twenty strong
swoops in breast near burst
with la-la gossip
gleaned from wilds upcreek.

On frenzied airtime
the droning year-end
committee reports
vie with twittered jab
at quirks and foibles
that thrive in thrushville.

While spitting grape seeds
from porch step to fence,
i lean strain to catch
some few distinct bits
of this ear-mocking
mighty crescendo.

At some muffled word,
what? i can't quite hear—
abruptly humf! whoosh!
the entire talkfest
lifts off as if bid
by a single brain.

Except one remains,
one bird abides calm,
unfluttered, unshook
in the tree's great void,
half-smile evincing
still centermost Point—

but what did he say?

Behind Each Mask

Halloween masks lurk and stalk:

Pirates under the live oak,
space cadets, battery-lit brain,
two ninjas, one giant cat
with pet witch, a squawking crane,
ramrod-stiff much-sequined queen
beside twins on pogo sticks,
kids threaten tricks if no treats
or fancy treats for no tricks—
good clean mischief and blackmail.

Yet, in this town the kids' fun
is preempted by fright night
for grownups costumed to seem
exotic, outlawed, adored.

Splashy masks gather in droves
plunged headlong toward milling swirl—
dead earnest this party time
spent outside the norms that set
their usual style hair and heart.

At least one night let's pretend
i'm Guinevere or Lancelot,
Crazy Horse, Empress Ci Xi?
antique painted chamber pot,
Babe Ruth? black leather bike dyke,
a lanky corn-on-the-cob?
anything not to be stuck
like a bug in resin blob
paperweighting the boss' desk!

Disguised to disclaim, disown
the daily victimized sigh—
a new mask might change its mien
if not menu or venue.

Behind each mask slinks a self
convolutedly inbuilt
hoping not to glimpse up close
that very same grownup schnook
it hadn't wanted to become.

No doubt (great sages assure
and some sixth sense may agree),
prior to this personhood,
its parentage, pedigree,
thousand motives, chain effects
from impulses overlaid—
behind each unmindful me
muddling thru this masquerade
shines the original Face.

Nearside Hill

Creek bottom's expiring sun
sets the gold poplar ablaze.

Glowing mist on frosted field,
under peach and nectarine
circles rich with fallen gold.

Dwelling years in the same place,
its features so familiar:
trees, rocks, grass, ducks and old barn,
the same tools, same chores, same walks.

Simple sights always in eye
yet how often overlooked!
I gaze blankly or speed by—
suddenly it springs to view,
the thing's been here right along.

Sure, i'm influenced at times
to dream astray, trip elsewhere,
lust hard for ventures and scenes
on the far side of the hill
thought needed for self-esteem.

Feats and sights on the far side
that informed folks warn Don't miss!
my dear. Haven't been there? Deprived.
At least i could then shout Done!
and cross a line off their list.

Sobered ponderosa-like
by shorter south-slipping days,
the huge dark pine overhead
flames up an instant pure gold.

Again desire rests content,
tomorrow like yesterday
exploring the nearside hill.

It's not how much i look at
but how acutely i see.

The Acorns

My accomplishment of recent afternoons?

To collect the acorns of local stalwarts,
the blue, black and live oaks, sort out the malformed
least likely to sprout strong, then shoulder my cache
around the nearby hills, place each an inch deep
tip up— i aim its tiny leap toward the sun—
in favorable ground of its own eco-niche.

Unlike the fictional 'man who planted trees',
no hero will succeed here in bringing forth
a thick woods where none stands. Hardpan is hostile
to root growth— i finish planting out my bags—
yet despite all hazards, a few will survive,
these seedlings under whose shade i'll never sit.

Special Work

                        Wisps of cloud,
curlicues way up. At the back porch
where unobstructed gusts hit club-hard,
only one yellowing leaf still clings
to the lilac clump. On the south side
elecampane stalks that sunburst high
over the common-run garden sprawl,
now topple composting into earth
made moist by early storm. In front beds,
even there not much to pick and pack—
maybe a few seeds, the several herbs
look too tatter-torn for tea, not much
above ground can prove this season's worth.

Yet relook! What's matured underneath?
below ground? Don't lay down tools too soon!

Ah, that must be the message friend owl
came hooting so grave yesterday dusk:
Time for autumn's special work. Dig deep,
uproot, wash off the dirt, slice, spread flat
to dry, then carefully store, and share
so that next year brings more.

A Two-Man Saw

Tools valued in bygone age
(not so long ago, that age!) rest here in rust,
rest unheld in pieces, yet let's hope in peace
for work well done by hand and foot, ox and horse—
bygone age.

Sad to greet one staunch homestead pal
propped against the shed, a rustic artifact
these days instead of indispensable tool,
a two-man saw, a brash crosscut toothy grin
no longer flashed while ripping clouds of pine dust
that sprinkle tangy scent over mounting pile
of winter's firewood.

Neglect is not its fault;
nothing broken, still cuts great— but where are men
with sweaty palms to grip its handles? to oil
its blade? to file its teeth? A willing workmate,
comrade at pull-pull, needing my proffered help
as i need his?

Today's prospective workmate
is sweating blood afterhours at indoor gym,
flexing hard-bulged muscle groups to 'stay in shape'
on some stud physique contraption. A machine
that neither works nor plays, generates no gain
of food or fuel, that can only fail to match
the body's own cell-born satisfaction when—
it did cut wood.

Widen and Pave

Our old dead-end single-wide lane served just fine
as it was. Well-banked, well-curved rabbit raceway
where two-leggeds could toe mud becoming dust,
or drive down seasonal ruts weaving past bumps.

To widen and pave. Such presumed improvement
indispensable for human habitat
gets imposed on our yet woodsy-type locale,
despite no resident wanting slick exit
pell-mell to shopperland. Now installed gape-mouthed
a half mile away, this noxious asphalt strip.

Says county officialdom: Roll out the black
carpet for your future neighbors who can't build,
mustn't build a home, not one! till this lane's brought up
to civilized standards, that is, to new code
mandating congestion-free infrastructure
(and profits at the in-laws' construction firm).

All noise of crunch on gravel, all chance of tire
touching nature-made substance must come to end;
all curves must be straightened to facilitate
tailgating our much-valued rural lifestyle.

Says my recurrent daydream: An army corps
of engi-deers deploys in prancing platoons
wielding their steel-encased hooves as jackhammers
to bioremediate this asphalt strip.

Brand-new road. A blink of geologic time,
perverse blacktopped thought-form. In weeks acrid fumes
decrease, its shiny surface dulls. Reddish dust
sifts across, gray sand fans out streaks when it rains;
by winter earth-brown mats of wet moldy leaves
draw scalloped artwork along the strict straight edge.

After a year depaving starts. The first blow
struck not by backhoe but by spongy puffballs!
modest fellows. Civilly disobedient,
with sun-loving vim they swell and press and ram
stick-to-itive heads right up thru the roadbed,
leaving a ring of quite depaved crumbling holes.

Hop, skip, jump. Elated speeds my evening walk,
for these little puffball musclemen give faith
that some forms of life will outlive the pavement—
altho not species Homo suburbanite.

IV

Who Is Native?

Pull the pump? Drat. Rain falls hard. There's no convenient day,
no right season for this miscreant machine to flunk
its task filling the water tank. Soon all hundred feet
of tubewell innards lie stretched across the field. We'll get
very wet fixing— tho i muse downcreek, yesteryear,
when gold-obsessed not-native folk once rushed to displace
the few native. With impetuous tromp dug up, sluiced, chopped,
ravaged the creekbed, yet settled here to own, to build,
repair, restore, perhaps relearn. Can these foreign folk
find a way to belong? restride the boundaried land?
reconnect to native state?
                              "Hey! Narun! Take the truck!"
as i fetch his pipe wrench on foot from the upper barn
(simpler, even quicker route), instead of bouncing wheels,
flinging mud around the fenceline. "Ya gonna do things
now the way a white man should?"
                              Indeed, why cut high weeds
peasant-style with hand-held sickle? Why move garden dirt
bucketsful two by two? light piles of brush with dry moss
(and a match, i don't rub sticks) instead of his fuel oil?
trim off pine limbs with a bowsaw? Less hurry, less noise
lets our brain absorb the land. Return to native self,
return to native state, i discover, must involve
happy recognition that a softer step is best.

Five decades back, acreage on the former wagon road
got split and sold. Only roof then was a dingy shack
long inhabited by two elderly lady-sorts
(rugged originals) who laid in piles of canned goods
each wintertime. Piles. No place to dispose of used cans
except out the side door, where accumulation rose,
monument-like, two lives' worth heaped up, twenty feet high,
still mounting at death. An honest seat, enthroned atop
while buried under their own self-consumed refuse pile;
regards to that near-extinct backwoodsy native breed.

Or, making a comeback? Once native in valley niche,
considered transplants this far upstream? emigrant stock?
(yet everyone arrives from somewhere else somewhen past)
anyway, in my first years, beavers had this floodplain
expertly engineered. Amid the blackberry wilds
their aqueduct contoured down the far side to keep ponds
brimful no matter how low the creek dropped. Leafless woods
would reveal occasional big trunks felled by big teeth,
bare willow stems neatly trimmed that otherwise would clog
their waterways.
        The hundred-year flood that rips down loose
every ten, moved so much gravel, it silted the ponds
and tipped the creekflow this side. Three new houses? their dogs?
spills from upstream sewage plant? Our beavers disappeared,
yet recent signs of trimmed willows— do they sneak back home?
reclaim native ground? reintroduce their native blood
to convert the neighborhood? It only takes one drop.

In town, on stately old mansion row, yellows and reds
fade to grays and browns; palm-size maple leaves blow to rest
smelling pleasantly damp. But whose nose pokes holes in sky?
prances right down the sidewalk (clickety concrete clack)
to stake out bold lease on winter domain. Stand aside,
each and every! Here comes the native son. Huh? Who dares
hold steamy nose as high as mine? The proud-antlered buck
hops a white picket fence and stamps with challenging snort
across the posh-kept croquet lawn toward a rival stag—
this other, tho, placed here for looks, a century ago?
cast-iron fake.
        Only a bulldozer could budge 'him'
or a crane lift 'him'. Yet our intrepid buck huffs Charge!
locks horns, twists, yanks, heaves. Combat rages, evenly matched,
shove, shove. One leaps back. Victory! The replica stag
topples to turf. Toward the loser a disdainful glance,
nose again in sky, our buck prances down the sidewalk;
yet after several strong hands figure how to attach
ropes, pulleys, hoist the vanquished tall to dignified pose,
replant 'him' foursquare, loyally rooted to the land—
i'd wonder, who is most native? Not this iron stag?

New Year

A dusting of snow
the night at year's end—
may it drift and sift
covering tucking tight
under goosedown quilt
the burdensome past.

And let me sleep late—
no! review, retrain,
revive limp resolve,
renounce laggard gait,
knead out creaky knots
crimping erstwhile hopes,
reinspect defeat,
reinstruct desire,
repolish furbish
plenish dim dull goals
that infuse value
into smallest act . . .

And after a spell
retooling myself—
watch, attend, be glad,
praise this all-agog
new year proceeding
so-so like the last.

A White Hair

Damn! A white hair—
not sun-bleached, not pale trustworthy brown
posed backlit— it's really white. Since when?
and here, another. Ow! got to pull
each root out. What if too many? Ow!
but why on me? Perhaps if reversed,
if repulsed— temporary downswing—
vitamins, megadose— can decay
once be unthought? Not supposed to hit
so soon. Ow! definitely white. Ow!
it hurts, tho less my scalp— until now
i saw only someone else's prized
lifetime running short.

Rough Gruff

                    "Colder than a well digger's ass!"
growled at many a midwinter afternoon outdoors,
the season when warmth had ebbed from the ground, and the muck
had churned two feet deep under hoof beside the old barn—
growled the same phrase more often it seemed as he slowed down,
perhaps needing to feel justified to stay indoors
where he hated to rest during the day. "Life's no fun
unless gettin' some job done;" his seven-day workweek
slipped to six, no vacation itch; "useless to go snooze
on some fool tropical beach."
                    Never knew what it meant,
that cussing phrase, i suppose a somewhat colder cold
derived from a deeper deep? than the grave digger's ass
is chilled by— tho mine heats up fine digging a tree hole,
just imagine a well! Our five-foot-wide creekside well
still used for the old cabin got dug before my time—
anyway, he cherished such down-home expletive yuks
to bolster his bossman build. A bluff rough gruff effect,
a gnarly shotgun-toting rancher stance, tongue-in-cheek
vigilant at gate and fence; gravelly grunts to prevent
affection's glint being glimpsed; yet if grouchy not grim
even in his later ill health.
                  His abusive shout
welcomed to intimate circle, announced a home voice
permitted what tone he pleased— the trick was not to duck,
certainly not to steel against assault, just to stand
upright empty of defended self-space, so his shout
could pass right thru. Then he felt relaxed. He only sought
the delight of throwing his weight around without whop!
hurting anyone— the rough gruff a fact about him,
sure, but not the truth.

Midnight Flakes

Blast of hail
rattling riff
bounces Jai!
snare drumming
on tin roof.

Ear alert!
rat tat tat
beebee-size
hurtling hordes
jolt dense-wall
skull-ceilinged
constrained nook;

quake mind-stuff
daily heaped;
break thru plans,
likes, moods, traits,
past deep-stored
brainstem needs
to core-craved
want essence
of all want.

Shake-up call!
frenzied blast
gusts down fierce
piercing pings
till sea breath
huffs out spent,
drumsticks' roll
slacks off soft,
one last plink
fades faintly
to hushed pause.

Then outside
billows white
my heart-cave's
timeless-aged
vision dream:
storm swirl face
whole grace reach
eye shroud hair
space one bond
all-embrace
rustling slight
seeks entry
at bedroom's . . .

Midnight flakes
bright spatter
the dark glass.

Yellow on White

Eyes greet a dawn-glowed inscape
as yet unhandled, untrod;
immaculate chaste mantle
spread glossy smooth overnight
obscures rotten stump, trench, road,
all muddy workaday stain.

Only one dried grassy stalk
pokes above the pasture's glaze;
each glitter-stacked pine needle
inclines low to let dislodge
gluey blobs; hollow thumps rise
beneath ponderosa boughs.

Across broad unmarred vista
the earth gleams pure like the sky.

Cloudlets shoot out wide awake
from my several cleansing puffs;
five steps, ice diamonds crunch crunch,
then a sizzle cuts jagged
yellow on white to bare dirt—
my first peehole, a new day.

Free-Form Verse

Ahh, near dawn, no urge to rise, could not— pressed close
under immovable sleep-abandoned weight,
my finger dips in astral ink and begins
to write across her shoulder blades free-form verse
better than brain invents— careful! keep these lines
untangled square to spine so that i can read
them later— or as lumbar lines tend to slant,
may i trust memory to groove deep each phrase
and play it back as free? not interpolate
its own version of what here occurs direct—
while day-mind awakes, catch up! scribbling like mad
my finger arrives at curved coccyx full stop.

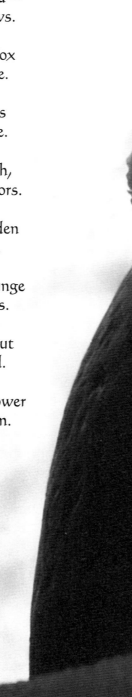

Home Heating

Arctic air has snapped—
cold wave, record lows.

Each single-housed fox
seeks a snugglemate.

Even vowed hermits
pray for goddess fire.

Snow freezes on path,
drifts high against doors.

Crept down deep in den
huddle furball folk.

Lights flicker, then plunge
corners dark for days.

Candle lamps drip out
while we try to read.

Chill-beating stove power
retreats to front room.

Too much of the pile
is uncured green wood.

In only one way
are things well in hand.

Boon! the ready-fueled
home heating device.

Breath steams, thick twined curls
cling damp in brown beard.

Creaking bones unbend,
blood throbs crown to toes.

This conjunctive stroke
sure beats chopping wood!

Varied gentle, hard,
the rhythms unforced—

Linga's energy
doesn't use itself up.

Delicate Smile

Cold soon-stormy noon:

Fragile, even frail
in features and face,
this pansy offers
multihued pensées
not just spring or fall
but in dry scorched months,
and now melting loose
from snow a foot deep
still blooms quite unfazed.

Weather-proof, deer-proof,
a one-year planting
that hasn't quit in two.

Among us tough boys
unready for fact
'pansy' meant puny,
a sissy— avoid
the weak at all cost!

Today having met
evidence, i've grown
to appreciate
her delicate smile
that conceals— no! stems
from her unimposed,
unassuming might.

She-Fox

Stroke of bad luck? an accident? an ill wind
that blew this morning, at cock's crow, that enticed
me to set greedy foot inside this mesh box;
the smell of meat, the lure of quick treat sufficed—
near-fatal mistake.
                          Wire door tripped clanging shut,
i leapt back, in vain, too late. My only crime?
circling the duckyard on my side of the fence,
presumed to be planning— what? No birdribs prime
stolen, no raid on the lard.
                          Let him approach,
not see me panic, pound frantic bloodied nose
against wire, not hear from me vixenish plea,
tho my big brown eyes glow with reproach. To pose
as protector of poor downtrodden ducks, nyah!
this trap isn't fair. Why, it's not proved i'd made vow
to poach.
                          Stroke of good luck! This man isn't the boss,
vicious in varmint war, who shoots on sight pow!
just for eyeing his ducks. Hurried, he left town
forgetting to check the trap. This other chap
looks more simpatico. He sits down. He talks:

"Look, She-Fox, i don't make the rules. I must clap
trespassers in jail, minimum twenty-four,
without bread or water. On these hills abound
permitted prey, rabbit and quail. I'll be back
tomorrow."
                          He slept badly, expecting sound
of complaint, whimper, whine. Not from me. I slept
grandly in jail, no toss-and-tear-fur, no wail,
tho wary, ready for? this body is caught,
why thrash? I could tug bang wriggle struggle rail
gnash at fate—

Morning. He's back. He sits. He talks:
"Look, She-Fox, thank stars for such a penal night,
this chance to ponder what neither comes to be
nor ceases to be. What abides untrapped, right?
at core free, must know to live free. Don't be shoved
rue-at-heart down the path of return! Learn well."

He reached out, fumbled at the hinge, rocked the cage,
i shrank tensed tight in corner. Wire-mesh door fell
ajar. One long moment i studied his gaze;
his chin gestured Go! Past his hand i streaked! flew!
heard no door clanging shut, paused halfway upslope,
glanced around. He squatted still.

                                  Can it be true?
door ajar? I-appearing-me free in fact
to roam uncaged? Not just hope idealized;
new-found mode sinks in. A condition inheres,
not won for self, but revealed and realized—
a freedom that ever is.

                        I shiver shake
after these hours crammed in terminal tight space,
resettle my coat, properly fluff my tail,
sniff deep, and lope away from that duckyard place.

Rivulet's End

          Run! Spun from evening walk—
pails pouring sweet-salty sky-fizzed intoxicant drink
trickle down chin, splash above boot tops, drip thru raincoat,
spill loads of washed-off wish belongings in pool flowed full,
then churn a sinuous rivulet slicing pert crease
thru raked-up pine needle pile clean to hardpan red dirt,
a canyon cleft being carved across my window view,
cherished window west where she one winter used to sit
and left a spot that lingers warm—
                            no, no, not bereft
in this world so caused that no energies can be lost,
all things merge in emerge from all things, or everywhere
is here, on simple reflection everyone is one,
meaning she herself is that She who teases the curl
of tropical storm runoff down hillsides' weedy hair,
swirling my yearning thru red crease into redder creek
colored earth blood from caved-in cliff upstream—
                                 vein-swelled flood
lifts up what once lay possessed, rips away delta-bent,
now surge-bodied sweeps on goddess-speed toward ocean womb
expecting rivulet's end.

Her Cloud Face

Winter sky painted a heavy-hued
drippy gray. Both hands mind the shovel—
my day's usual topsy-turvy thought
engrossed for now adding a tree hole
to the row along the drainage ditch.

Repetitive yet not boring work
to wiggle edge thru unloamy dirt,
butt against, scrape, stomp hard, then pry up,
stoop down and pitch out the rounded rocks
deposited by an ancient stream.

Excited, a flicker's orange flash
points look! I glance up to startling blue.

Aii blinding! One great radiant cloud face
   explodes west, its backlit rays ablaze,
   flaring white-crested cumulus burst
   come penetrating, a laser shaft
   translumining my opaque self-stuff.

   Merciless keen thy sword-twirling gaze!
   unsoothing thy touch! no sighed relief
   felt in thy discomforting embrace!
   o fire-spewing hundred-and-eight-named
   crazy Lady. Obliterant bright.

   Her tangly-tressed spangly sunbeam hair
   whipping clear the gray in my heart's wind.

   Yet upwells: Ma, save! protect! guide me
   by safe degrees, guard from disarray—
   preserve this moment! fix fast undimmed
   thy sun-eclipsing gaze— please bestow,
   i implore— do what's benign. Ma, stay!

   Unpossessable, her cloud face fades,
   that Devi by whose shining all shine.

   Composite face, sum of each i've met
   or never once glimpsed or still may greet,
   emerged from formless to old-new form
   looking so much part, so much the heart
   of my world— even if disappeared.

   Both hands mind the shovel. Stomp again,
   wiggle this edge down between, pry up,
   stoop low, wrestle out embedded rocks
   which obstruct the root zone— keep digging,
   keep digging, the tree hole's almost dug.

A burn day. Every day now a permitted burn day
with crisp skies, brisk breeze to whisk smudge away. Time to burn
the accumulated litter of autumn decay:
rampant-run blackberry vines, broom brush, broken oak limbs
blowing down yet from that deep snowfall four years ago,
waist-high heaps of pine needle mat. Stack branches, hack brush,
rake firebreak in squares or curved mounds contouring the slope
above the ravine.
     Strike one match! Spread to many fires—
what's ready to burn, may it burn! A spine-zinging rush
as orange flame spurts thru gray smoke. Crackling tongues lick out
blackening each rake-patrolled jigsaw piece to its edge;
not a thing left unblazing beneath big yellow pines
but the rake itself, flicker-lit by arms' rhythmic flick
hundred times repeated. All else here to ashy dust;
all reduced to primal prior state. The very ground
billows and glows. Burn up what must burn!
       As dark descends,
more pine needles heaped on mounds jetting flame. Tho i rake
downhill not up, it's soon warm— coat off— finally hot—
glance around. No wonder! Flame is torching my rear,
how did that pile behind me get lit?) scorching the cloth;
crinkling skin comes next. Drop the rake! Bolt! Make zigzag streak
to the water trough beside the barn. Dunk sizzled butt;
soothe well in slimy brew. Fortunate, whew! No one's there
risking a split side.
     My compadre arrives to share
the quiescent phase, when fierce spark-hurling flames die down
to docile gleam underneath crust, settle calm like cows
eventide chewing their cud, ruminating on space
but in order, grassy space prepared to sprout anew,
clutter cleared, green stuff that sputter starts blazed clean to ash,
shape-age-name reduced to void.
      So be it! As without,
so within. Give to fire the patter, the chatter-mind,
the accumulated litter of unease, pursuit,

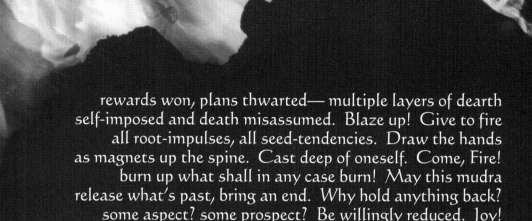

rewards won, plans thwarted— multiple layers of dearth
self-imposed and death misassumed. Blaze up! Give to fire
all root-impulses, all seed-tendencies. Draw the hands
as magnets up the spine. Cast deep of oneself. Come, Fire!
burn up what shall in any case burn! May this mudra
release what's past, bring an end. Why hold anything back?
some aspect? some prospect? Be willingly reduced. Joy!
self-accretion to ash. Svaha!

In response to chant
invoking by ancient names the all-igniting Eye,
the dancing flame-ringed Heart, one died-down pine needle pile
springs to life! In response to chant jets out bright blue flame
thru its dull burnt crust; darts to incinerate each bit,
each offered bit of self-stuff. Again the chant intoned
reverberates in the ravine. Another relights!
this pile also the past hour looking done. Draw the hands
up the spine. Cast from inmost depth. Svaha! Sparks flash high!
eager to welcome, to cherish, to incinerate
each offered bit of self-stuff.

Once invited to work,
fire initiates unrelenting process, probes and points,
extends its long long inreach, may hide under dull crust
yet shoot forth so urgent . . . When everything that can burn
has been burned, what remains? Would that some jubilant Soul
rise dazzlingly jeweled from ash. Rather, tho, It abides
quite still, a seeming nil. No acclaim. No aim. No name.

Heading North

Gray misty autumn morning:
with weary downbanking whir
he landed plump in our pond.

Winging south thru valley fog
this youngster had lost his skein,
his route, then heard barnyard fowl.

Once here, unhurt but worn thin,
his bulk filled out, sheen restored
by our caregift of cracked corn.

Appreciative tho didn't speak,
kept apart, never belonged
to any one cackle clique.

Most migrant web-footed folks
joining domestic gaggle
gladly come in from the cold.

Yet dedicated bhiksus
who journey toward all-one-bond
leave home "like geese from their lake."

Spring morning, the hills fresh green:
an approaching airborne din,
his own, a skein winging north!

Five months he hasn't flown a beat.

No mulling over the choice,
with exultant honk! honk! honk!
he's instantly up and gone.

Born wild, born for heading north—
the direction adepts face,
the direction of release.

Allergic Sneeze

Sun rising brings breeze,
then shorter breath and allergic sneeze
from yellow-green sticky alder haze
drifting off creek bottom puff upslope
to tickle nose oversensitized
because long acquainted— but don't flee!
don't move away!

I won't seek new home
just to sniff elsewhere some blooming tree,
get stuffed up, obstructed, once more moan
about the boredom-racked lack of wine,
cuddlemate, or song.

No! stand my ground!
not that i own this piece, yet i'd own
the urgent need to be realized
as One who abides unmoving, Here,
beneath behind pity-begging yelp
and bullyragged snarl.

Moving wouldn't help
dense-pressed reactive globs disappear,
couldn't point the way out this mind-groped maze—
even if i had lives more to roam
Ma Earth searching for that perfect spot,
finding which i'd inspect life a lot
while not growing fast allergic, nope!
to the next scene's resnuffled go-round
born of pollen-seized reprised me-mine,
same old me-mine.

No Plops Allowed

Cow's pasture at winter's end:
wild lettuce thrives juicy green.
As i stoop over to pick,
broad inquisitive noses
amble up to poke around.

"Hey! Out of my salad, back!"
i wave a sergeant's finger
under their grass-perfumed chins.
"And don't dare make any plops
in my pristine lettuce patch!"

No plops allowed here, no mess,
no flops either, nothing botched,
nothing goes wrong— Verboten!

Spring Is Here!

Dawn is clear.

Workman sun's
huffing haste
mists off grass
frosty white.

Three red-cap
lusty charged
woodpeckers
bam! bam! bam!
tap tattoo
on phone pole.

"Ya, ya, ya,
of of course,
no bark bugs
in this pole.
We've to call
our flatland
relatives
with the news
it's winter's
last last freeze.

"They'll be glad
to whiz up,
oh, next week,
late to catch
crystal glint
on creekside
twig and blade,
but in time
to to claim
nesting rights
and admire
sun sun-fed
daffodils
facing south.

"Why, we'll all
gather round,
share breakfast
pecking talk,
warm our bills,
then sortie
att tack tack
those bark bugs."

Spring is here!

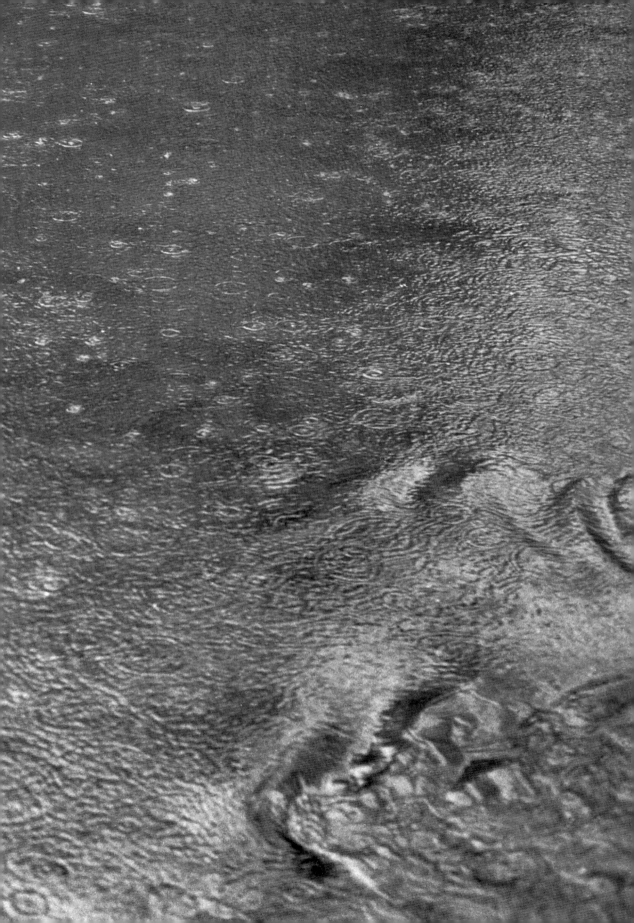

Terms and Notes

14   *Seismic Stomp*   How did i so forget? In this realm of forgetting everyone has forgotten who the 'I' really is. The truth of oneself inheres prior to all the various layers of misidentity. A remembrance [Sanskrit: *smṛti*] that cuts thru mere memory is the way to realization indicated by the Veda-derived philosophy called Vedānta.

       Or, recollection in the sense of all-round attentiveness [Skt: *samyak smṛti*] is given by Gautama Buddha (565-480 B.C.) as the seventh aspect of his eightfold process. The second aspect is right intent [*samyak sankalpa*], an all-involving resolve that subsumes and transcends habits of discipline, personal choice, development of skills, and projected goals.

       This mythic beast (in the photo) joined me at the handicraft bazaar, Nairobi, Kenya, on New Year's 1960. Hundreds of deftly crafted lions looked just like lions; only this one looked like the old Kikuyu woodcarver who brought it forth. Its mighty roar has filled my living space, or for some years my sister's, ever since departing its native savanna.

17   *The Mother Space*   Jai! [Skt: *jaya* victory, triumph] is used as a jubilant salutation. Hail! Praised be! Well done! Hurrah!

19   *At the No-Exit Spot*   Altho the self-entangled psyche finds no way out, as in Jean-Paul Sartre's drama *No Exit* [*Huis Clos,* 1944], the field of awareness manifest as oneself and other is ever free. And is itself the way out.

       I shan't! In appropriate usage 'will' indicates the simple future in first, second or third person; 'shall' indicates a special resolve or query. This distinction is muddied by our contraction 'i'll'; neither 'won't' nor 'shan't' sounds like its auxiliary verb. Additionally, nineteenth-century British grammarians introduced a nonhistorical artifice, switching 'shall' for 'will' in the third person. This prissified usage reached our shores thru the efforts of schoolmarms to make their new-world students sound proper. Americans therefore avoid the stilted tone by not using 'shall' where needed. We must reclaim it! We shall!

26   *Reluctant to Stop*   Sunrise and sunset impose a natural pause to be marked in the day's rhythm. Its observance in Euro-American village life was called the angelus. A bell rang from the church steeple. Everyone stopped. Even now in many towns the bell still rings. But we don't stop. So i blow a conch shell to strike a line under daywork.

28   *Jousting with Info-Glut*   Mistaking windmills for giants. Despite having had to cross the language barrier, this comic-tragic image is so widely known in English that we hardly remember to thank Miguel de Cervantes for *Don Quixote de la Mancha* I:8 (1605).

36   *Chinaman*   "A finger pointing at the moon" is the oft-referenced simile in Chan/Zen tradition for a teacher's function of pointing at illumination, at the abiding Light. Without the finger to point out Look! we may well miss it. On the other hand, the master cannot guarantee transporting anyone to the Light. Each of us must attend to our own innerwork.

46   *So Near*   *Love's Labour's Lost,* a comedy by William Shakespeare (1564-1616). Here's a chance to acknowledge his untold numbers of phrases and images that form the basis of figurative speech in modern English. How to write a few lines without the old boy reaching in?

47   *Name-Tagging*   In our current usage 'thou/ thee/ thy/ thine' have unjustifiably grown obsolete tho not quite extinct. I don't intend any poetic or ecclesiastical tone. These second-person singular forms express familial, youthful, or intimate relationship. Does any other language try to dispense with this essential function? Oddly enough, the plural 'ye/ you/ your/ yours', used for courteous address at the beginnings of modern English, has now deteriorated into the impersonal object 'you' with no subject 'ye'. 'Thou' is used with the second-person plural verb: thou walk (not walkest). 'Thy/ thine' is used like 'my/ mine': thy artwork is thine.

48   *She Is*   Among Śakta poets into whose tradition i was formally initiated at age 28, the most unequivocal voice is the Bengali Caṇḍīdās (?1410-80). His songs are kept current by the Baūl

sect of wandering minstrels. The passionately embraced paramour Rāmī is worshiped simultaneously as the all-transcendent Goddess whose body is our entire world. The Beloved is both veiling and revealing force. Each woman incarnates Her in a special sense; birth in a female body carries that benediction and that obligation. Culminating the troubadour tradition, a similar devotional search for himself in Her, the Creatrix as embodied in his amour Laura, is lived by the Italian Francesco Petrarca (1304–74). See sonnets 47, 104, 123.

Triangles. A deity-diagram [Skt: *yantra*] represents female potency by interlocking triangles that radiate from the male center Point (Omneity) thru stages of concretization causal to astral to physical (Activity). Whatsoever we can experience is Herself, the One Mother.

52 **Rush for Refuge?** The rope mistaken for a snake. A well-known analogy in Vedānta illustrating the usual state of misperception: five senses register an object, mind draws a conclusion. However, what the mind presumes to be true is not.

Force at base of spine. The action of moment-to-moment attention, at most moments inattention, is portrayed in Tantrik Yoga as a coiled-up serpent [Skt: *kuṇḍalinī*] that wakes or sleeps according to an aspirant's effort and attunement. Egg-shaped space. The etheric field [Skt: *prāṇamaya kośa*] electro-magnetized at arm's length around the physical body.

The place or person of refuge, the act of taking refuge [Skt: *śaraṇam*] is the basis of conventional strategies for salvation. At some stage it may no longer serve the necessary encounter with oneself.

54 **Ancient Gods** Below! Above! Beyond! / That, the Source, the illuminating Sun, / the Truth we adore and contemplate; / may It enlighten our questing hearts. [Skt: *bhūr bhuvaḥ svaḥ / tat savitur vareṇyam / bhargo devasya dhīmahi / dhiyo yo naḥ pracodayāt. Ṛg Veda* III,62:10, tr. Narayan]. Popularly called the Gāyatrī mantra, in the 24-syllable meter called *gāyatrī*. The root utterance of Vedic culture; perhaps the oldest preserved utterance of humankind. All-pervasive, all-inclusive Light, symbolized by the sun, is invoked at sunrise and sunset for the blessing of everyone. For millennia its chanting has celebrated the wide community of aspirants and the continuity of endeavor to share this quest.

Jai Indradev! [Skt: *indra* chief; *deva* celestial] Victory to the Rainmaker! Thunderbolt Hurler! Ruler of the Skies! Equivalent in other Indo-European cultures to Zeus, Jupiter, Thor.

58 **This Twosome** Void [Skt: *śūnyatā*] has a renunciatory connotation as the emptiness of everything desired, but also means the fullness of everything once desire is released.

60 **Young Kitty's Case** Kālī [Skt: Black, Time-as-Destroyer, the fierce bloodthirsty Goddess; pronounce ā as in father, ī as in feet].

63 **Error of Scale** Change at one's core occurs not by passage of time, but by intensity of gaze that encompasses oneself as a whole, rather than as an assemblage of parts. Looking, listening without the conflictive desire to change or be changed. Appreciation here for a lifetime's ever-challenging dialog with the teaching-demonstration of J. Krishnamurti (1895-1986). For example, see chapter 24 "On Time" in *The First and Last Freedom* (1954).

68 **One Thru-Flow** Prickle-pin lips, clamped jaw. Breathing release as an intentional therapy requires a helping hand to keep the reclined patient inhaling thru the symptoms of shutdown, the muscular cramping called tetany.

76 **Autumn's First Touch** Are questions a nuisance to be solved by resorting to conclusions? An aphorism i found in Nietzsche (1844-1900) served my student years: "A very popular error: having the courage of one's convictions; rather it's a matter of having the courage for an attack on one's convictions." [tr. Walter Kaufman, *Friedrich Nietzsche*, 1950]

78 **Heron House** Unerring aim. The same lesson from observing the same bird 2600 years ago: "Who can wait quietly while the mud settles? Who can remain still until the moment of action?" [Lao Tsu, *Tao Te Ching* 15, tr. Gia-Fu Feng and Jane English, 1972]

84 **The Longer Reach**   Today i don't feel to reach so high. At the birth of lyric poetry in the Greek Aegean, Sappho (?620-565 B.C.) writes of her immediate personal sphere: "at the tip of the topmost bough / the apple-pickers missed it. / No, they didn't miss it; / they couldn't reach it." [tr. Jim Powell, 1993] Are they supposed to? Our prevailing cultural assumption sees only self-assertion and clamorous action as leading to success.

86 **No Right System**   In longer-line poems about rock walls or fruit harvests, we tend to hear Robert Frost (1874-1963). No specific content in this poem relates to any of Frost's; his largely iambic pentameter is not my metrical model. Yet here's a place to acknowledge a shared temperament and procedure. The poet as Everyone walks into the woods alone and learns something important about self and world.

90 **Behind Each Mask**   The original Face [Skt: *svarūpa*] as a koan is attributed to the Sixth Patriarch Hui-Neng (638-713) whose *Sūtra* in Chinese is fundamental to Mahāyāna. Does any culture not understand the mask as metaphor? And we wear not just one or two!

95 **The Acorns**   "The Man Who Planted Trees" (1954) is a pretend-historical short story set in his native Provence by the novelist Jean Giono. And let's remember the nonfictional northeastern pioneer and orchardist Johnny Appleseed (1774-1845). Long live the trees!

110 **Yellow on White**   Bumpkin humor punctuates the haiku of the impious Zen hermit Kobayashi Issa (1763-1827). "Pee-hole pocked leftover melting snow." [*Cup-of-Tea Poems,* tr. David G. Lanoue, 1991] No ideal exists apart from the real; no unmarred vista defines the perfect.

111 **Free-Form Verse**   Merci bien to the goddess for loan of her back! I find a vague memory of the same picture in a poem by Johann Wolfgang von Goethe (1749-1832) that i would have read in my college years. Salutations to his effortless but precise musicality, which became my aesthetic standard. And to his evocation of the Ewig-Weibliche [the eternal Woman-Presence].

112 **Home Heating**   Linga [Skt: sign, symbol]. The upright stone represents the Ever-Aware, the still Point, the irreducible One, Spirit as masculine, standing in the Yoni [Skt: womb, source], the Ever-Creative, the exuberant Profusion, the immeasurable Many, Nature as feminine.

116 **She-Fox**   Even today's overdomesticated adult brain should be able to engage the energies and attributes of our various animal selves. Our most thoroughly shared cultural food is the fairy tale read to children but meant for adults. This folk heritage from Aesop (600 B.C.) to the Grimms' *Fairy Tales* (1815), Burton's *Arabian Nights* (1888) and many others worldwide was collected from word-of-mouth, or newly composed as serious literary oeuvre. My foxification of the human dilemma may remind of Jean de La Fontaine's fables in verse (1668-94) which passed into all European cultures via the nursery. A fox was his favorite character. "She-Fox" is however not a fable; it describes an actual event.

120 **Her Cloud Face**   Ma! [Skt: Mā] is the call for Mother in all Indo-European languages. Devī [Skt: goddess, from *div* to shine; pronounce e as in tray, *ī* as in feet].
    Digging, digging, dug. "Making, making, made" was an oft-repeated phrase uttered by the widely venerated Śrī Ānandamayī Mā (1896-1982), in whose physical presence i sat in the mid-1970s. Sporadic practice becomes an unbroken current, effortful yields to easeful, the sudden enters the gradual, in course of self-direction supervenes an All-Power that itself directs.

122 **Blaze Up!**   In the fire ceremony [Skt: *yajña,* the basic rite of Vedic culture] all egoic accumulation, one's unaware nonessential self is offered up using mudrā [Skt: seal, gesture] and mantra [Skt: seed-sound, sequenced phonemes]. Svāhā [Skt: joyful exclamation, perhaps from *sva* self + *ahā* ahah! also the ritual oblation; also the Goddess of offering].

124 **Heading North**   Bhikṣu [Skt: mendicant who lives off alms]. "The mindful consider no place home, but take leave without regret like geese from their lake." [attributed to Gautama Buddha, *The Dhammapada* 7, tr. Narayan]

128 Spring Is Here! In Hermann Hesse's novel *Steppenwolf* [*Der Steppenwolf,* 1927] the ascender type is cracked in fragments by his lifelong effort to project himself into the Ideal. Passing midlife, Hesse was given a garden property where he then exercised a different kind of effort. Years outside, hands in the dirt, less involved with writing projects, not "constructing the hundred-gated cathedral of Spirit," rather connecting mind to the actual, the thing-as-it-is. A leaf, a bloom, a root, a rock. Things not formulated by thought. "The many" not flailed at like an obstacle, rather lovingly described and allowed its "transformation back to the One." See the poem "Hours in the Garden" [tr. Narayan, "Stunden im Garten," 1936].

Gifts Received

Palms join together. The author wishes to express utmost appreciation for— well, everything. So let's begin with ancestors. They crossed the ocean whether storm-heaved or becalmed; they crossed the forest primeval; they crossed sagebrush basin and alkali flat; they found the continent-wide trails. And along the way most of them would perish young. How to honor in our current safer journeys those not so long deceased who took such risk? How to follow in such footsteps?

Two names received. The first from my father's grandfather Charles, woodworker and inveterate hiker, who with his daughter taught six grandsons to explore up willow-lined creeks away from bustling streets into far-open vistas. The second name is from my mother's father Guy, who rode horseback the last unfenced rangeland, saw his frontier vanish, then helped his preacher-clan wife raise four daughters to be culture-loving, town-dwelling ladies.

Sharp sunlight, expansive horizons. Add the gene for persistent inquiry. Or maybe it's a bug. Both my parents had it. As educators they demonstrated the inborn itch to find out, not to rest satisfied with half-baked answers; they shared the process of ever-new learning so as to remain lively thruout life. My own version of inquiry turned from the world as it appears back to the self that registers its appearance. Yet my mother Marilee and my father Alvin have wholeheartedly supported my lifelong quest along tracks and sidetracks not often their own.

What is this always pressing matter? this not quite evident All-in-One? In earlier years i went native on five continents, living with families or fellow students who spoke assorted tongues (French, German, Amharik, Malay, Hindi). Later i pursued opportunities to engage many renowned and many unpublic teachers, to absorb ancient wisdom systems and modern instruction pointing at the No-Thing. During this innerwork i received a third name, Narayan, as an indicator. It reminds. Tho soon i learned, above all, that within everyone of any race or faith, underneath our differing concepts and constructs is shining an essential goodness, an inherent truth. Not recognized, however, unless we undo our programmatical nowhere-rooted mind.

Time then to sink my own roots. But where? I grew up near that beach-and-car zone where most everybody has recently come from somewhere else. Back to the land! Feet on the ground! Grow native in the westslope foothills. At first it didn't feel more like home than anywhere else; many places around the globe have felt like home. No, by staying close i've made it home. Only occasional calls have taken me away for a while. Now wanderlust expresses itself in age-old pilgrim fashion, on foot, backpacking without a tent, up canyons, months trekking the Snowy-Toothed Crest— but there's another story.

Typeset in Bitstream Calligraphic 421
and printed on acid-free paper
by Hignell Book Printing.